Be Your Own Decorator

Be Your Own Decorator

Taking Inspiration and Cues from Today's Top Designers

Susanna Salk

RIZZOLI
NEW YORK

New York · Paris · London · Milan

Introduction

By Susanna Salk

This is not a how-to design book, but a *why not* book. Why not finally create the kitchen that feeds both your appetite and soul? Why not finally fix that living room layout that hasn't felt right since you moved in? It's not about having enough time or money or the right phone numbers to call. It's about understanding that taking stuff out of a room (even if it was a wedding gift!) is sometimes as important as what you put in it. That the eye delights in seeing multiples and gets bored when things look too matched. That character beats price in the beauty department hands down every time. That the biggest rule of all is that there really are no rules, except to be confident about your choices.

I'm not a designer. But people often compliment me on the unusual color of my walls or an arrangement along my fireplace mantel. The credit shouldn't be paid to me, but rather to the dozens of designers who give me confidence, to the ones who put stylish rooms together that feel grounded yet never take themselves too seriously. If I do anything well, it's that I'm not afraid to try their ideas and configure them into my own space. I think of them as indispensible style sherpas, helping me find my way and then leaving me to enjoy the view.

Designing our homes is one of the few creative ventures where we can—and should—draw ideas from the pros without fear we'll be branded a plagiarist. A room that borrows its balance from design dean Billy Baldwin's uncanny sense of proportion is original: the room's owner has plucked and inserted borrowed ideas into her nest like an inspired magpie.

Translation is never literal in interior design, but rather lyrical, with new notes being added to each incarnation, a gift that keeps giving ad infinitum, always ripe for reinterpretation. The soothing color of Martha Stewart's hens' eggs inspired her to build a whole paint collection around them (Mother Nature being the original creator). I, in turn, copied those very same shades Stewart featured in her magazine for my son's bedroom. My painter liked the effect so much he lifted the same combination for his kitchen, but added a darker ceiling. And so on.

Often I have used the images in these pages when verbal descriptions proved insufficient: when it came time to build a fireplace in our new house, I showed a picture of Washington, D.C. designer Darryl Carter's kitchen fireplace to my mason and he immediately understood what I wanted when I said "modern traditionalism." Whenever it's time to choose a new color, I lean on the genius daring of Miles Redd for moral support. (If Miles can pair pink with red in his living room then I can paint my mudroom tangerine!) Even when I get dressed, the designers are cheering me on: one look at the work (and wardrobes) of Los Angeles-based uber designers Kelly Wearstler and Mary McDonald reminds me that glamorous accessories are as key to a room as they are to an outfit, so choose a lamp with the same witty reverence as a bangle.

And now it's your turn. This book is about emboldening you so you can embolden your rooms. I want you to be inspired rather than intimidated by my most favorite rooms from some of the best designers and tastemakers around. While many of them already showcase their work in their own wonderful books, I wanted to gather a unique compilation under one roof and categorize them by what they do best: whether by breaking rules or being whimsical. Consider this book and my determination your own personal design guide.

It doesn't matter if you don't live in a Hollywood bungalow or a Connecticut colonial. The idea here is that it's about echoing a spirit rather than a swatch. When I breathlessly relayed the title of this book over the phone to American design master Albert Hadley, I feared he might find it disrespectful. There was a long pause after I finished, then he replied: "Well, I think that idea's just marvelous!"

Hadley's genuine enthusiasm for educating those not fortunate enough to hire his services was shared by every designer I spoke with. Unlike many artists in other mediums, interior designers never hoard their secrets. They are a gloriously generous bunch, much more concerned with making the world a more beautiful and livable place than worrying about whose idea it was to put that vase over there. So be inspired not only by their work, but also the spirit in which it was conceived. Stop worrying that you won't get it right and realize that perfect rooms are boring. Rooms that resonate with personality—not rules—are the ones you'll want to linger in and savor.

I hope *Be Your Own Decorator* will help you decorate your home with your own personality. Whenever you do this, you can't go wrong. Because in the timeless words of innovative designer Dorothy Draper: "I believe in doing the thing you feel is right. If it looks right, it is right."

Color

The right hue not only impacts
the room's décor, but also your mood,
so never underestimate its power!

Colors can't clash. A simple glance outside our window at nature's infinitely interesting combinations is reassurance enough that it's really just our preconceived notions and fears about what goes with what that often prevent us from finding the hues that will make us happy. Color is about feeling and rooms that haven't yet been introduced to their proper color will never fully function as they truly should. A chilly blue in a kitchen is never appetizing. But tangerine? Suddenly everything feels yummier right down to the menu. A pale yellow in the master bedroom can feel sadly institutional, yet a golden butter tone makes you want to linger between the sheets longer and conquer the new day with optimism.

So throw out everything you thought you knew about color—whether it dons your office walls or refrigerator door—and instead, focus on how it makes you feel. Then gravitate towards those shades even if at first it feels like they are not "allowed." If you are still unsure, you can tread behind these designers who blaze color trails and slash through myths with the zest of early pioneers. You'll start feeling freer about exploring uncharted color territory.

Worried big colors only work in big spaces? It's actually the opposite, as so elegantly proved by Alessandra Branca (pp. 50–51), who infuses life into a little sitting room with a shot of rhubarb red. Think fuschia is too hot for a dining room chair? Not when it's elegantly paired with wood and white, according to Angie Hranowsky (p. 47). Tired of bland beige? You'll never weary of Rose Tarlow's living room (pp. 28-29), where various shades of it strike a harmony that is both complex and serene.

The colorful rooms that follow are proof positive that every color works as long as it's paired with confidence. So if you're like most people and scared to dare, then borrow some inspiration here, until you find your own. Just remember, rather than a color wheel, let your feelings be your ultimate guide.

Color is

Beige with creamy whites create a room with a soothing sense of serene luxury.

Strong colors on curtains give a room instant depth and drama.

A surprising color on walls, such as turquoise or violet, can provide an appeal that is both sexy and sensible.

Color on an accent wall gives tricky rooms personality and panache.

Yellow tends to get regulated to the kitchen, but it's much more sophisticated than we give it credit for!

Try punctuating with pops of color through accessories. It's like putting an exclamation point at the end of a sentence.

"I wanted to take this grand space and make it totally livable," says designer Bunny Williams. "I always try to mix the humble with the grand. For example, the curtains are inexpensive Italian bedspreads! And at the other end of the room—reflected in the mirror—is an over-the-top eighteenth-century bookcase into which we put a flat screen TV. By combining comfortable furniture with bold and rand color, the room felt old world and brand new at the same time."

Design by Bunny Williams

In a bedroom refuge she designed for a client, Alexa Hampton cleverly kept extraneous
costs down by creating dummy curtain panels and then tucked the blackout shade behind the valance.
Meanwhile, the intense use of yellow in different hues and patterns gives
an intense feeling of luxury.

Design by Alexa Hampton

"While I like living and dining rooms warm and cozy, I prefer bedrooms and bathrooms to be cool," says Miles Redd. "The pale blue and gray paired together here becomes a cool and airy retreat from the rest of my apartment. And I love how the bed canopy and curtain valance play off each other."

Design by Miles Redd

Butter yellow makes the ultimate feminine backdrop for a portrait, almost becoming its own frame into which to set a painting. The orange lampshade continues the glow and makes the space both vibrant and tranquil. "This retreat was designed for a young, newly married couple," says designer Robert Passal. "The concept was to create a youthful, exciting space that they would be able to grow with."

Design by Robert Passal

Master colorist Jamie Drake dresses his rooms like a fashion designer, with equal parts drama, restraint and style. Here, turquoise blue is the star accessory.

Design by Jamie Drake

The use of purple in a study has a surprisingly masculine effect when combined with leather-paneled walls and painted wood. The graphic rug keeps the mood strong from the ground up.

Design by Katie Ridder

Who would ever think to bring a pink, orange and blue color palette into a 1940s barn? Designer Eve Robinson did and this sitting area is the better for it: "The space was very dark when we purchased it so by painting the original cedar walls white, we brightened things up," says Robinson. "The whimsical use of natural elements and colors from nature—whether of a sunset or sky—give the room a modern yet warm vibe." Stone was added to the façade of the brick fireplace to give it texture and depth.

Design by Eve Robinson

Warm woods paired with creamy whites and beiges give Rose Tarlow's grand living room a serene, cocoon-like effect. In the spring, Tarlow welcomes vines from outdoors to grow directly in, thereby rivaling her other treasures to be the room's most elegant accessory.

Design by Rose Tarlow

"Since this house is historical and quite grand from the outside, I wanted the interiors
to be classic, but with a fresh twist to suit the sensibilities of the young family who lives there," says
designer Melissa Warner. "Mixing classically lined pieces with a bold
color palette let the furnishings match the grandeur of the house, yet still be approachable.
I enveloped the entire space in the brushed metallic and ivory wallpaper to give
it a soothing, yet interesting backdrop. The tall, ivory tufted headboard is dramatic
and the scale of it makes the room feel more spacious."

Design by Melissa Warner

Violet and white make for an elegant pairing in the living room that feels as open and inviting during the day as it does moody and glamorous at night. Rugs and cushions are an especially easy way to bring in pops of color while still keeping the overall scheme clean and serene. "I played up the purple and the pattern in this room, but I was careful to not overdo it," says designer Angie Hranowsky. "I pulled out the more subtle beige tones in the rug for accent fabrics and wall coverings."

Design by Angie Hranowsky

Goodbye Picasso

Maureen Footer used the striking yellow bindings of *National Geographic* magazines to give this summery sitting room all the cheerful light it needs.

Design by Maureen Footer

In this sunroom, Kristin Gallipoli wanted go over-the-top with bright colors to make the space welcoming. "But I also wanted it to be as comfortable as possible," says Gallipoli. "To do that I found a vintage sofa, which I stripped to the bones, filled with down and had my upholsterer make one long cushion instead. Perfect for naps!"

Design by Kristin Gallipoli

You don't have to use many different colors in a room to deliver a unique impact. Often just two will do. Using white in a large space has a presence as strong as any darker hue and yet gives the eye plenty of room to luxuriate. The hearty texture of the rug, coffee table and fireplace basket keeps the layout grounded, while the white door and the oversized secretary blend into the back wall to allow the turquoise of the artwork to be the room's showstopper. More threads of blue in the curtains and sofas ensure that the focal point isn't tipped too much in the painting's favor.

Design by Carrier and Company

In their classic antique Connecticut farm house, designer Carol Bokuniewicz and
her husband John Smallwood wanted to honor the integrity of the house yet not get too country. Here,
at one end of their dining room, the floors—a patchwork of different periods—were stained white
to bring a unifying effect with a Scandinavian undertone. "The walls then begged to be dark," says
Bokuniewicz. "It makes for a wonderfully dramatic effect in the evening."

Design by Carol Bokuniewicz

A strong envelope of color is very forgiving when it comes to low, sloped ceilings and here it enlivens a quite dark room.

Design by Carol Bokuniewicz

For a ten-year-old girl, designer Betsy Burnham wanted to create a room that was more teenager than childish: "An all-white kid's room would be the last thing anyone would think of and so I went with that!" says Burnham. "I then added sporty, Adidas-style stripes and a crazy custom chaise." To top it all off, Burnham took the vintage chandelier from the dining room, painted it red and hung it in a corner.

Design by Betsy Burnham

Unexpected color combinations help create a vibrant, inviting space. Deep, rich colors (such as navy blue silk on the walls, the rust wool embroidered drapery panels and the bronze of the chandelier) all make the room seem to glow with a sensuous, glamorous vibe you'll never tire of seeing.

Design by Geoffrey De Sousa

Peter Dunham's first New York apartment (before he became a professional decorator) was a [...] with cheerful bright yellow paint and the floors with wall to [...] piece counted. The windows were left bare as they [...] detail worth displaying.

Peter Dunham

Wanting her bedroom to feel both traditional and fresh, designer Diane Bergeron transformed a small room with an industrial feel into a romantic retreat, thanks to the pairings of gray silk and large-scaled orange toile. "Don't be afraid to use color," advises Bergeron. "As you can see it does not detract from the room's ultimate sophistication."

Design by Diane Bergeron

COLOR

In her own dining room, Angie Hranowsky creates a space that can stylishly accommodate her children as easily as dinner party guests, by using a hide rug that is both magic-marker and red-wine proof. The white tulip table is a stylish foil to the fuchsia silk chairs and the turquoise stools. The salon-style art wall is a great way to engage an expansive wall with the rest of a room's décor and give it instant personality.

Design by Angie Hranowsky

Inspired by the water outside their windows, Steve and Brooke Giannetti painted a white guest room a deep teal blue. "But the blue was a bit too bright so we sanded it, which then gave it a great chalky feel," says Brooke, who made inexpensive headboards by covering wood in washed burlap. "We also brought in an antique Gustavian chest whch works beautifully as a bedside table and provides extra storage. Every room should have at least one antique."

Design by Steve and Brooke Giannetti

With no real windows, this tiny sitting room was brought to life by the bright color and by mixing toile and chinoiserie in the unexpected colors of brown and pink. "The brown suits a man, and yet at the same time, is very feminine," says designer Alessandra Branca. "The yin and yang of decorating is so important!"

Design by Alessandra Branca

Maximize every area in the bedroom and treat your linens and curtains almost as another wall to be painted. Here, distinctly different—yet harmonious—wall, curtain and bed linen colors, all work together to set off a unique bed frame and create a mood that feels both exotic and comforting.

"The best thing about growing up can be the transitional stages," says designer Thomas Beeton of the room he created for a twelve-year-old boy. "I kept the scale modest, leaving plenty of room to still spread out on the floor for games or sleepovers. The primarily black-and-white scheme with the punch of Yves Klein blue on the chaise makes it easy to coordinate with bedding and accessories and looks cheerful and sophisticated day or night. The bold stroke of adding the Sputnik-esque light fixture finishes it all off. That can remain through the high school years into college days!

Design by Thomas M. Beeton

Mix

Every room needs that organic
juxtaposition of style, period and price point
to feel like it's uniquely yours

As a culture, many of us have been raised on the notion that only like-minded things belong together. Happily, the past fifteen years or so have brought a more mainstream acceptance to the notion that a Chanel jacket not only can be paired with jeans, but should be. And interior designers can be thanked for pushing the boundaries of eclecticism so that we are no longer surprised when Target coexists with Tiffany in the same room.

Mixing pieces in a room—whether by style, price point or origin, breaks the somnolent hotel room vibe so many spaces suffer from when they get too matchy-matchy. To create a really vibrant space, periods and price points should mingle and court one another. It's amazing how much better the very precious and the very cheap look when plucked out of their comfort zones and placed side by side. Who really wants to sit in a room full of only expensive antiques anyway? Or, for that matter, top-to-bottom modern?

Milly de Cabrol knows that a pillow of a British flag can cohabitate alongside an 18th-century French armchair and a suzani-style textile because they all share one thing in common: her all-abiding affection (pp. 84-85). For Nate Berkus, a graphic black-and-white rug is the ideal foil to set off—and also unite—faux bamboo chairs, modern art and mismatched, cosy reading chairs all inside a vintage 1929 Chicago building (p. 99). And New York designer Katie Ridder (pp. 80-81) mixed her clients' Swedish antique chair and inlay tables with fresh coral and lavender color accents in a way that gives the revamped room a decidedly modern twist.

How do you know what to put next to what? Most designers would answer that when every object or piece of furniture has a reason for being in the mix, then it will all work. And sometimes the best reason for including a piece can be simply because it is loved.

Mixing is

Mix is a prerequisite if you want a room that feels vibrant—and this doesn't just mean furniture. There should always be a variety of wonderful objects to discover around a room.

An intense juxtaposition—such as a whippet-slim modern chair with a vintage wood table—or a zebra rug in a country setting—can work if the arrangement is given a dignified, thoughtful placement in the room.

The surprise of a colorfully painted wall can be the ideal backdrop to signal an elegant anything-goes atmosphere.

Shake up sedate older pieces by placing them in an unexpected way. An ancestral portrait goes from sleepy to sexy and reupholstered antiques catch a modern vibe.

Mixing in strong textures with quieter pieces gives a sexy, substantial feel to any room.

If everything in your room has a personal meaning then the mix will be an effortless success.

Stephen Shubel designed his 17th-century pied-à-terre as a neutral backdrop and perfect tiny frame for his personal treasures. "The eighteen-foot ceilings and grand windows with dreamy light were the key to all of my inspirations," says Shubel. "Bathing everything in white paint and adding wall-to-wall textural sea grass helped to expand the proportions."

Design by Stephen Shubel

By painting their living room ceiling and walls a modern robin's-egg blue,
Paul and Sara Costello create a space that feels distinctly fresh and expansive and allows them to
fill it with deeply personal treasures. There is an elegant fearlessness at work at every level here,
with pictures hung according to the heart and by combining the sumptuousness of the mirror,
chandelier and fabrics with the simplicity of a bare floor. As a result the eye is thoroughly entertained
yet never intimidated.

Design by Paul and Sara Costello

"My clients have three little boys," says designer Brad Ford. "They also love to entertain so I wanted to create a room that was casual, but still felt sophisticated." While keeping the color scheme monochromatic, Ford mixed in a variety of natural materials and textures, which gives a large space dimension and interest. "I also made sure that all of the furniture was low maintenance and kid friendly."

Design by Brad Ford

MIX

Lulu de Kwiatkowski has fun surprising her guests with an up-tempo mix of heirlooms of her past with creations of the present. "I think in a guest bedroom you can be a little more playful," says Kwiatkowski. "The old master painting is from my husband's family, the bed sheets are my design and the pink chair belonged to my grandmother who was named Minerva. It all adds to the spirit of the room!"

Design by Lulu de Kwiatkowski

Mixing vivid color with a combination of unique frames
(all with a symbiotic old world feeling) gives a wall more than enough personality to
stand up to a sofa already full to the brim with character.

Design by Carol Bokuniewicz

This kitchen table was designer Carol Bokuniewicz's desk for years until she moved it into her kitchen. "Used office furniture stores are often a great source for good vintage stuff," she says. "I always respond to pieces with strong distinctive graphic forms as they anchor the space."

Design by Carol Bokuniewicz

MIX

To give a rustic room a lighter, more modern feel, Eddie Ross and Jaithan Kochar used slightly overscaled, wow pieces—such as the bust, candles, black shade and zebra rug—to make a small living room feel grander.

Design by Eddie Ross and Jaithan Kochar

"I wanted to make toile interesting and current," says Melissa Rufty. "The unique color combinations really reinvent such a traditional pattern. And people often shy away from hanging art on toile but I say don't be afraid to embellish the pattern with groupings or larger pieces."

Design by Melissa Rufty

New Orleans native Angéle Parlange has always been enamored of turquoise, so that was the hue she chose to paint the living room walls of her Manhattan apartment, thereby giving it an instant exotic lift. "With that bright backdrop, I kept the furniture mostly neutral, although still interesting," says Parlange. "And the pink pillows keep things fun and flirty."

Design by Angéle Parlange

Who says a sun porch has to be filled only with wicker and stripes to serve as a summery retreat? Here, eclectic art (whimsically hung right on the shingled wall) make this unique room feel connected to the indoors; the chic shades of turquoise, cherry red, orange and butter yellow—combined with Italian wrought iron furnishings and bold florals—celebrate summer's palette while making the most of a space that easily could have been forgotten.

Design by Jay Jeffers

"The concept for this house was Caribbean with a modern edge," says its designer Angie Hranowsky. "I pulled the colors for this room from my research on Matisse's Moroccan period." All of the hues in the room also tie back to the bottle cap portrait, including the brass accents. The combination of modern Bertoia chairs and handmade free-form wood table all work beautifully atop the cotton dhurrie rug.

Design by Angie Hranowsky

Celerie Kemble adroitly mixes colors, periods, shapes and accessories full of personality without overdoing. Despite walls upholstered in a chocolate shagreen and hand-painted moldings in an inlaid bone pattern, the exotic feel of the room is much in thanks to the shape of its tufted crescent sofa, built to fill the entirety of the room. Because of the lack of pattern on its upholstery, the eye is allowed to focus on its playful lines, pillows and positioning of the painting just above.

Design by Celerie Kemble

MIX

"I wanted this half of my living room to not look too decorated," says designer Joe Nahem. "Instead, just a compilation of some beautiful and unpretentious pieces. I felt the room could handle the strong blue hide stools, as it was in a small dose, and on a moveable piece of furniture."

Design by Joe Nahem

Textile designer John Robshaw thrives from juxtaposing the treasures he brings back from India (such as the hanging textile, the barrel chair and wood table) inside his weekend home. "I love mixing the tribal with Connecticut country," says Robshaw.

Design by John Robshaw

"I wanted to combine the owners' antiques and artwork with shapely silhouettes of furniture to create a sophisticated, unusual color palette," says Katie Ridder, who painted the lavender wall with a pearlized finish to give it a lift.

Design by Katie Ridder

No matter the budget, a room can have a luxurious feel when glamorous colors, textures and surfaces are layered with highly visual—and personal—artwork. Here the charcoal and black hues of the pillows, the bed frame, the picture frames and the lamp lend an organic formality.

Design by Ryan Korban

Design by Darryl Carter

"My goal when I created this room was to engage the sensibilities of the wife who is a modernist with the husband's who is a traditionalist," says designer Darryl Carter, who made the antiques feel approachable by upholstering them in linen. "Linen is always a great foil to accentuate the architecture of an antique furniture piece while instantly updating it," says Carter. "Period damask would have made the room feel too stilted." Now the room seamlessly honors the past while managing to feel very of the moment.

Design by Darryl Carter

"I wanted to highlight all the colors I love—strong pinks, yellows and burnt oranges—and use them everywhere, particularly in the Moroccan carpet," says designer Milly de Cabrol of her living room. She also loves to combine styles: from a mid-century coffee table beside a colonial arm chair to an 18th-century French armchair. "Cohesion comes with confidence," says de Cabrol. "I don't worry whether things will go. If I love them, then they will."

Design by Milly de Cabrol

Every great room—no matter its size or function—is filled with objects that tell a story. In photographer Oberto Gili's Italian farmhouse the narrative is eloquently told from the moment visitors enter: from an American-flag long board that caught his eye on a trip to California (and now hangs like art work) to the roses freshly snipped from his garden, to stacks of pictures from a recent shoot, everything has a meaning, a memory and, therefore, resonance.

Design by Oberto Gili

"It's about a devotion to objects, a fearlessness when collecting and curating that is both high and low," says designer Stephen Alesch of the unique knack he shares with his wife, Robin Standefer, for the art of arrangement in their home. "It's not about being stagnant; it's about only buying the things you love and making sure they don't match!"

Design by Roman and Williams

"The Moroccan lamp in the foreground was the initial inspiration for the exotic feel I wanted to create," says Sean McNally of his living room. "I started looking at books on Moroccan decorating and noticed that a lot of the rooms consisted of furniture that was lower to the ground so I followed that direction to create an intimate feel. The artwork is an eclectic mix of paintings of flowers in vibrant colors found at New York City flea markets and what I have come to call my 'Indoor Garden.' Flea markets are a great place to find those special one-of-a-kind items. Figure out the story you want to tell first, then make it as strong as possible for a big statement."

Design by Sean McNally

Flanked by a pair of salvaged house columns, the 1740s farmhouse living room of designer Annie Kelly and her husband photographer Tim Street-Porter is dappled with pieces with large personalities such as the seventeenth-century English chairs, oversized creamy ottoman and red lampshades from Target. The striped rug from Pottery Barn not only unifies the space but also draws visitors inward with its cheerful personality.

Design by Annie Kelly

"This is my own home, and I wanted a great nighttime living room that envelops you and is still comfortable," says designer Melissa Rufty. "It's rich and cozy with a deep high gloss lacquer on the walls and multiple seating areas conducive to intimate conversations. And I hung artwork underneath the sconces to create a more inviting space. Unlike most people's formal living rooms, the space actually gets used."

Design by Melissa Rufty

Matthew Patrick Smyth knew this corner in his house could dazzle guests as easily as it could provide repose for reading the Sunday paper, so he squared off the long, narrow space with a furniture layout that makes the most of the dimensions and natural light. While the sofa is free standing, its careful measurements give the impression of a built-in window seat. Meanwhile, a fabulous and unexpected floor covering warms the slate floors.

Design by Matthew Patrick Smyth

When Robert Stilin wants to get comfortable, he simply indulges in his iconic 1958 Arne Jacobsen Egg Chair, which, when combined with the raw, untreated wood of the nearby fireplace mantel and the power of the photograph above it, feels as modern and exciting as if it were just created.

Design by Robert Stilin

MIX

For his own Chicago living room, designer Nate Berkus had to make a large space feel intimate. After assembling a variety of vintage pieces over time, he thoughtfully arranged them in a manner that allows for elbow room. The pair of bamboo gold chairs centers the room and ensures the singular pieces are appreciated individually. The whole mix is kept lively by a graphic rug and modern art.

Design by Nate Berkus

To make her New Orleans an ode to the iconic designer Billy Baldwin, Valorie Hart painted her living room a similar (yet slightly softer) shade of the brown of Baldwin's famous Manhattan apartment. To address the room's asymmetrical proportions (and unable to afford an eight-foot-high Chinese screen she craved) Hart took old shutters and placed them in front of the inconsequential window, instantly creating a moody backdrop. A vintage camelback sofa with Chippendale legs becomes worthy of being the focal point when it's reupholstered in faux white leather and nail head trim. "If you can afford to buy the best, do it," says Hart. "But of you can't, don't freak out. Just get creative."

Design by Valorie Hart

Design by Valorie Hart

Valorie Hart mixes a rustic vintage metal bar cart and distressed antique mirror with luxurious lime-green silk drapes to bring a feeling of bohemian grandeur to her room. To further personalize her treasures, she painted a bust of a lady bright orange to echo the bright orange chandelier.

Arrangement

It's in these little landscapes amdist
the room's grand scheme where we can
truly express ourselves

The art of arrangement isn't about whether this chair goes here or fretting that a shelf of books is all lined up properly. It's about placing the objects with the greatest emotional importance center stage regardless of their price point. It's about understanding that anything grouped together takes on the importance of the collective whole. (It's also about getting creative with the very things that display the objects, as they too play an equal part in the art of the artful arrangement.) It's the difference between creative clutter and chaos—a fireplace mantel lazily jammed with framed photos does not an arrangement make—and understanding that editing out is as important as editing in.

For John Derian (p. 119), a casually overstuffed arrangement of deeply personal photos and cards in his Manhattan entry hall makes for a kind of ever-evolving sculpture, especially when set against the wallpapered backdrop of pages torn from old books of poetry. For New York designer Charlotte Moss (p. 129), her office is the opportunity to pay a formal homage to women she admires, with an elegant arrangement of black-and-white portraits expanding across the blue-and-white floral wallpaper as if to say: "Welcome. Women make a difference here." The art wall adorning Kristen Buckingham's Los Angeles home (pp. 122–123) brings a flat space to life with its vibrant collection of lithographs, photographs and vintage oils arranged like a casual gathering of favorite friends around a dinner table. "I just wanted to have fun with it," says Buckingham. "Last-minute inspiration turns heads all the time." When it's done right, arrangement displays the personality of the arranger as much as it does the objects themselves.

Arrangement is

Pictures can be hung and stacked on a variety of levels and surfaces all at once.

Arrangement in a working space doesn't mean corporate: after all, where is it more important to be inspired than in your office?

Frames don't have to match nor do their contents need to correspond. Their sole purpose is to capture the eye.

The unique spot where things are gathered and arranged can contribute as much to the power of the display as their contents do.

Bookshelves can be sexy!

A bit of nature is always a welcome addition to the mix.

ARRANGEMENT

A bull's eye mirror helps expand a small entry space while the vintage engrave and cast-iron antler hat rack give it an extra shot of personality. This is an eloquent example of how every nook in a house can go far in expressing its owner's spirit.

Design by Matthew Patrick Smyth

THE IRISH W

108

ARRANGEMENT

The enchanting gaze in this portrait of a girl reminded Amie Weitzman of her own twelve-year-old daughter, so she gave the painting a central location in her living room and allowed its personality to shine by keeping the art work around it diminutive in size and less striking in color.

Design by Amie Weitzman

109

"We love black floors because they are rich and reflective and make the floor feel like the ocean at night," says designer Robin Standefer of the floor she and her husband Stephen Alesch share in their Manhattan loft, which is full of places for creating. "The gloss adds a lot of life."

Design by Roman and Williams

نقطة ماء

ARRANGEMENT

When creating a gallery wall, Caitlin Wilson wanted it to be an eclectic and personal mix that had an element of surprise: "I love that the wall is random yet balanced," she says. "I carefully planned the layout, which can be done by buying a big roll of kids' art paper and tracing out different options. It's helpful to take swatches of your fabrics for the room and have some of your frame or matte colors coordinate to give a sense of cohesion."

ARRANGEMENT

Design by Caitlin Wilson

One man's castoffs are another's gold: Eddie Ross and Jaithan Kochar salvaged this built-in cabinet from a Brooklyn street and set to fill it with beautiful, useable things for their country home. "Choose a color palette and stick with it," suggests Ross. "Then layer in varying surfaces and shapes. We even spray painted the pottery matte black to look like Wedgwood Basalt Ware!"

Design by Eddie Ross and Jaithan Kochar

A bookcase can provide a room's biggest drama—especially when it acts as the perfect foil, not for books, but treasures of all sizes, shapes and colors. The key is making sure that each little stage provides its own story about the person who lives there.

Design by Catherine Malandrino

For those of us who worry that a wall must be perfectly painted and the frames upon it hung in exact harmony, all we need to do is simply gaze at John Derian's living room to understand how artful and beautiful imperfection can be.

Design by John Derian

117

Books—and their wonderfully haphazard arrangement—can play as much a role in giving
a wall personality as art (not to mention jewelry). Here, what could have been an empty corner becomes
a place that deeply personifies its inhabitant, to the point where you could probably pick her out in a
crowded room before you had even met her.

Design by Elizabeth Daugherty

John Derian makes coming home completely personal by displaying an overstuffed arrangement of mementos in his entry hall in such a way that its shape takes on a significance as poetic as the items themselves. Not to mention the wall, which has been coated top to bottom with hundreds torn from old books of poetry, so visitors feel as though they've walked into one of Derian's celebrated découpage designs.

Design by John Derian

Mary McDonald wanted blue instead of white for her office so its cool palette would be as
welcoming a space for both her female and male clients. To make an instant style statement on a featured
wall, McDonald first had cherry blossoms painted across the blue and then layered on her favorite
black-and-white fashion photographs in a manner she aptly dubs "premeditated whimsy." And for her
most daring gesture, she added a turquoise rug on top of the sisal to give visitors the fabulous feeling
that they have entered into the world's chicest Easter egg.

Design by Mary McDonald

When it came to creating her own gallery wall, designer Kristen Buckingham was fearless: "You never know until you try," she says. "Worse case scenario, you repaint or patch." Happily, in her case, the entire wall is as interesting as a whole, as each frame is individually. The sofa pattern is especially vivacious in order to draw some attention to itself.

Design by Kristen Buckingham

ARRANGEMENT

Tori Mellott defied the bland home office myth and instead created a space that is super chic and resourceful. Instead of bookshelves, cubby-like cubicles, (which feel open and gallery-like) display her invaluable collection of resource books, magazines and light-hearted collectibles in a tangible, inviting manner. Elegant lamps—fit for a dining room—paired on a white desk reiterate that the mission of this room is to be both inspirational and industrious.

Design by Tori Mellott

The inspiration for Gene Meyer and Frank de Biasi's bedroom was hatched after they found plastic African mats at a Monoprix in Paris and glued them to the wall to simulate the tiled walls they had seen while on vacation in Tangier, Morocco. When the bed of unfinished wood (also purchased in Morocco) arrived, it was promptly painted pink. The power of arrangement often comes by the understanding that combining what is beloved—instead of precious—is what captures the eyes and heart most.

Design by Gene Meyer and Frank de Biasi

A wall is given strength and history thanks to a well-edited and well-hung mix of art. The arrangement is given additional depth thanks to the continuation of the display on the bureau. The pairs of lamps and candles respectfully frame the bust, which in turn is framed by the powerful black curves of the mirror.

ARRANGEMENT

Richard Mishaan proves that you don't need to play it safe with art: why stop at hanging just one picture per wall? Here, a variety of frames and mediums bring life, texture and personality to a dining room that could easily have stopped at simply chic. The white chairs and rug allow the walls to shine, yet ground the space with their own distinct personalities.

Design by Richard Mishaan

Dormers posed a challenge in a guest bedroom, but ultimately, the designer Darryl Carter succeeded in creating a stylish reading retreat. "Don't be overcome by quirky architecture," says Carter. "Engage it."

Design by Darryl Carter

An office shouldn't be just a place to get work done, it is also the perfect place to reflect its owner's spirit, dreams and goals. Here, Charlotte Moss creates the ultimate feminine retreat for herself by hanging portraits of the women she admires for constant inspiration. It's the perfect example of the power of an arrangement that's based on emotion and is not just decoration.

Design by Charlotte Moss

A massive bookcase doesn't just serve to keep order, but becomes its own kind of wall sculpture by displaying books and treasures in a casual yet focused fashion. The sturdy, modern style of the case corresponds with the floor lamp and sofa both in color and spirit so that there's unity rather than distraction.

Design by Amie Weitzman

"What I love about this cabinet in this very casual room is that it makes a strong architectural statement," says designer Suzanne Kasler. "I like the grid design in the glass doors, so I was inspired to use the cabinet panes as a way to frame, and created individual vignettes within each. I like leaning pieces of art against the cabinet wall and using various textiles, colors, textures to make a statement."

Design by Suzanne Kasler

Jane Stubbs didn't worry about whether her beloved collection of 18th-century volcano prints [suited] her giraffe-patterned sofa and oriental carpet. She simply hung it with aplomb, and as a result the arrangement uniquely enhances her living room's fiery spirit.

Design by Jane Stubbs

For the design of his guest bedroom, photographer Pieter Estersohn adheres to the philosophy that decorating with less discipline is sometimes more, especially when the pieces have been collected by a world traveler. "I think if there is a cohesiveness to your eye it will all ultimately work," says Estersohn. "At the end of the day I don't see décor here, I see all the memories associated with the trips where I discovered everything. For me this is ultimately more satisfying than worrying about matching beiges."

Design by Pieter Estersohn

"Keeping the shelving off the floor makes everything feel lighter and more spacious,"
says Tom Scheerer of the entrance to his home (formerly a convent) in the Bahamas.
"The bookcase boxes were made locally and attached directly to the pickled
cypress paneling. It's a very functional way to store the heavy weight of books
without overpowering the space."

Design by Tom Scheerer

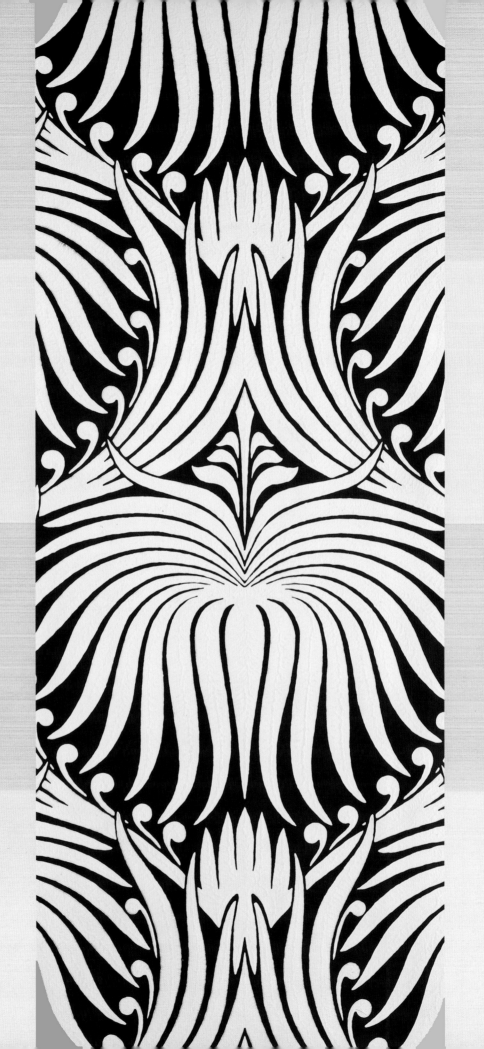

Balance

How to achieve harmony in your décor,
whether through placement or pairs, that feels
both soothing and spirited

It's a trait we consistently strive for in our daily lives, yet often forget that half the battle may lie inside the very havens we seek away from our hectic schedules. In other words: balance starts at home, not in your calendar.

How refreshing that for once, this longed-for state—both physical and mental—is something you actually can control, if you'll first allow yourself the little luxury of assessment. So often I walk into rooms that feel like a frenetic conversation between two strangers who aren't listening to one another: a lamp without a nearby mate here, a chair no one uses over there, or a sofa positioned so its main goal is simply to stare at a television screen. Take a look at your spaces as though for the first time: are the elements really engaged with one another? That doesn't mean they must be Jane Austen-ready for tea and proper conversation. Spontaneity and surprise can just as easily take place in a well-balanced room: if anything it provides a more composed space where the fun can begin.

The rooms that follow share a commitment toward completion. These rooms feel grounded because their foundation lies on an axis that resonates from floor to ceiling and wall to wall: sofas face one another in ways that promote conversation, not admiration. Mirrors and lamps have thoughtful partners. Architecture and accessories reinforce a feeling rather than attract attention to themselves. For Jan Showers (p. 147), the stalwart design of eight, uniform Louis XVI-style chairs allows a floor-length mirror to deliver all the dazzle without over doing. Harmony is achieved when Tobi Fairley (p. 146) creates a mirror image of bracelet chairs and over-scaled ginger jars in an entry way.

Again and again here you'll find that balance never equals boring. Although there are many ways to achieve it, the end result is always the same: rooms that can be lived in, rather than merely walked through.

Balance is

Curtains in solid colors can anchor a room and give it strength and depth.

The power of pairs, whether highly hung mirrors or low-slung sconces, can elegantly even out an active room.

Accessories or furniture, when in conjunction with color, harmoniously ground a space.

The repetition of color soothes a space, no matter the hue.

Bookcases on either side of a room's back wall can have a grounding effect that also helps to expand the space.

When one side of a room expertly echoes the other, the effect can be both chic and calming.

BALANCE

Windsor Smith achieves primary balance through the repetition of the room's ink blue drapes: "If I didn't bring that powerful stroke of saturated color to the space it would be too airy," says Smith. "They give the room a certain thunder." The double-sided couch in the center also helps achieve equilibrium by creating two areas for intimate seating. The accessories do the rest with aplomb. "There is no better way to balance a room," says Smith, "than to anchor it with a pair of something captivating like pair of bronze zebra ottomans!"

Design by Windsor Smith

BALANCE

Robert Couturier achieves elegant equilibrium not just by anchoring his wall with pairs
of stunning mirrors and other decorative objects but also via instinct and memory.
"While a room's décor can seem as if it had magically fallen into place, my instincts are
supported by the very many hours I have studied the classics and the moderns," says Couturier.
"Knowledge of the different styles, their ideal proportions and their relations with each other
are crucial to an effortless result. The more you know, the freer and the better you are."

Design by Robert Couturier

"A entry is like a great party invitation: it sets the tone for what's to come," says Tobi Fairley. Her goal in this particular one was to make a statement with color. "The room was fairly small so we had to make a lot of impact in a little bit of space," says Fairley, who choose the perfect coral with just the right amount of depth to it. "The mirrors were the finishing touch that really expanded the size visually."

Design by Tobi Fairley

Jan Showers expertly solved a distracting door and window in her own dining room by covering them with a mirror and then placing drapery and torchiere in front to create the illusion of two windows. Rows of dining room chairs lined in elegant precision lend a balanced crispness. "This is one of my favorite rooms I have ever done," says Showers. "I love how the dove gray of the walls plays with the golden yellow leather of the vintage dining chairs. You don't see these two colors together very much but the combination is so chic!"

Design by Jan Showers

BALANCE

To create a space that is well edited, designer Betsy Burnham made sure that each item
in the room had significance. "I wanted to create a room that won't go out of style," says Burnham.
"Color used in unexpected places, such as the pair of sconces over the fireplace, provides a great
twist and keeps the design fresh and balanced."

Design by Betsy Burnham

BALANCE

Charlotte Moss keeps everything masterfully balanced in this sitting room
(thanks to matching pairs of sofas, coffee tables and bookcases) but never dull.
Delicious pops of red bring delightful vivacity.

Design by Charlotte Moss

The first priority for Steve and Brooke Giannetti, when renovating this 1970s living room, was to transform its most overwhelming feature: the lava rock fireplace. "We wanted the room to feel like a timeless, waterside retreat," says Brooke. "So we covered the lava rock with white grout until it had the feel of an old stone wall and blended more with the rest of the room." Artwork with a unifying oceanic theme grounds the surrounding white and reminds visitors of the location.

Design by Steve and Brooke Giannetti

Ryan Korban creates a deeply personal bedroom by layering luxurious textures and strong visuals against an all-white palette. A synergy between the two pairs of artwork contains their shock value just enough to allow them to be appreciated on an everyday basis.

Design by Ryan Korban

BALANCE

By mixing warm and cool colors then layering in complex neutrals, such as rose-tone drapes and an eggplant sofa, Curated creates a balanced interior that also feels dynamic. "It's color without too much color," says founding partner Elena Frampton. The unique photograph above the fireplace is further grounded by bookshelves in warm wood on either side.

Design by Curated

How do you walk the tightrope of using over-the-top color and not fall off? Jonathan Adler understands it's all about employing the power of pairs as your guide: the dramatic sconces, whimsical wicker-elephant end tables and graphic pillows all ground the ecstatic color while still contributing to the fun.

Design by Jonathan Adler

BALANCE

A room with a spectacular view and proportions to accompany it should have an understated yet powerful and balanced décor that lets its best assets do the talking. Here, lots of white and chrome act as the perfect backdrop for the strong, industrial lines of a vintage factory table. Paired with the warm, wood tones of the Viennese chairs, the space feels both functional and special.

Design by Diamond Baratta

BALANCE

In the living room of this prewar Park Avenue apartment, David Kleinberg interplays antiques from different eras. "A great deal of mid-twentieth-century furniture is inspired by eighteenth-century models so mixing the two periods keeps the room from becoming static," says Kleinberg, who lacquered the walls in a high-gloss stone color to maximize the light. Artworks by Ellsworth Kelly, Willem de Kooning and Robert Motherwell are thoughtfully showcased in a reverential manner that doesn't overshadow the furniture and keeps the floor plan feeling balanced.

Design by David Kleinberg

BALANCE

"I wanted to make this bedroom feel like it was part of a villa on the French Riviera," says Texan designer Jan Showers, who achieved her goal thanks to the repeated sunny presence of yellow, which seems to radiate out of the gold-leafed Soleil Mirror above the bed and then around the room in elegant, grounding accents. The bared expanse of a glossy wood floor adds extra-glamorous impact and reminds you to think twice before unfurling that rug!

Design by Jan Showers

BALANCE

To get maximum play out of his Greek Revival farmhouse, architect Gil Schafer—along with designer Miles Redd—devised its public room to perform duo roles with equal importance: "Miles and I designed the big table to double as both a dining and a library table," says Schafer. "When I'm not serving dinner there, it's stacked with books." Schafer covered a very inexpensive table with a cloth and then cut holes in the table top (and the cloth) to run lamp wires down to plugs in the floor: "I dim the lamps for a soft glow at dinner."

Design by Gil Schafer with Miles Redd

"I wanted to focus on the simplicity of the extraordinary lines of the furniture here," says Mary McDonald. "But instead of creating a traditional seating group I paired identical chaises and pillows with a multipurpose ottoman to give cohesion."

Design by Mary McDonald

BALANCE

The shelves of collectibles are orderly without feeling fussy and cohesive without matching. Therefore, they balance the room without making it bland. While the designer Carol-Ann Speros' instinct was to keep the fireplace mantel in its original state, painted white, her client was passionate about transforming it with a dark finish. "I was so glad I listened to her," says Speros: "A happy detail like this can make a difference in how you feel about your finished project."

Design by Carol-Ann Speros

A custom-designed banquette makes the most of a difficult corner. "Most people just put a chest and mirror in a foyer," says Melissa Rufty. "But this was a great opportunity to do something more inviting. I love a banquette—it says, "kick off your shoes and stay awhile." Facing pairs of portraits and sconces give the lively mix some structure.

Design by Melissa Rufty

Whimsy

The power of the unexpected—it's every
room's secret weapon!

Touches of whimsy in a room cause us to pause, exclaim and wonder.
Whimsy can be executed many ways: via color, form or placement, but the
effect is always unexpected. Whether it envelops you the moment you cross
the threshold or tickles you as you get a glimpse of it gracing a corner, whimsy
adds ripples of excitement to a room.

Whimsy should never forget its place, however: its job is to entertain but
never at its host's expense. The rooms that follow all celebrate the big and
little ways to create a sense of discovery. And discovery is important to a
room—even when it's your own, you should never be able to take it in all
at once. Whimsy helps to involve us, inviting us to be a part of the room's
unfolding narrative. It also means someone cared enough to go beyond mere
decorating to create delight.

Christopher and Suzanne Sharp (p. 175), exemplify whimsy with one of
their uniquely patterned rugs topped by a fanciful and unforgettable green
chandelier, which feels like an exclamation point in their elegant dining
room. Whether it's the Novogratz family's (p. 191) eclectic treasures plucked
from their world travels (a Balinese day bed for lounging and an oversized
British flag hanging on the wall), or New York designer Kevin Isbell's kitschy
lobster lamps (p. 187) slyly winking at the room's seaside locale, whimsy is
what lingers in your head long after you have left for another place.

Whimsy is

Marvelous color in unexpected combinations in unexpected places can be chic: like tangerine and turquoise or black-and-white stripes in a bedroom.

Playful accessories, such as a snail coffee table in a Brooklyn apartment or lamps with lobster bases in a beach house, can surprise you and yet look perfectly at home.

Using whimsical wallpaper in small spaces expands the room's mood, whether it's swimming fish in a kitchen or dandelions and butterflies in a sitting room.

Arrange boldly scaled pieces in ways that highlight their presence: a 1920s bust in front of an abstract painting or tree branches placed like antlers on a white wall.

Experiment with putting things where you least expect them yet where they still serve a function: a picnic table in a city kitchen or an outdoor lantern inside.

Try hanging art wherever it pleases you: whether below waist level for unique impact or boldly above your bed in lieu of a headboard.

Suzanne Rheinstein wanted to give her client a bedroom that was both theatrical and glamorous. The high arcs of the canopied beds luxuriously draped in silk create special spaces within spaces (and beg to be crawled in to), while the contrast of the steel beds, raffia rug and painted walls feels chic and fanciful.

Design by Suzanne Rheinstein

Christopher and Suzanne Sharp make whimsy feel at home by infusing it into their dining room from the ground up. It starts with their lively rug pattern pattern, which is echoed, in spirit and through the repetition of its verdant color, in the chandelier above for a quirky balance. The fireplace mantel becomes another opportunity to express the Sharps' creativity and, like everything in this room, doesn't take itself too seriously. Even the wood is stacked in a lively way.

Design by Christopher and Suzanne Sharp

"This room feels like it has an old soul," says its owner and designer Kelly Wearstler.
"All the elements are like heirlooms from journeys across the globe. Their different textures and shapes
and unexpected color combinations coexist yet each has its own voice. It's important to create a dialogue
between the interior and the architecture and it can be even more dramatic if there are contrasts."

Design by Kelly Wearstler

"People are afraid to try color, fearing it is limiting but it's actually very approachable and can work with so many different styles and materials." Here, Kendall Wilkinson softens the heady punch of the turquoise-and-tangerine palette with a hand-painted mural, Lucite headboard and neutral bedding for an overall look that is both playful and ethereal.

Design by Kendall Wilkinson

"I am very sentimental about things," says Harry Heissmann of designing his own home. "It's to the point that the items I place in a room become my 'friends.' I find things everywhere. I think emotion and involvement are important tools in creating a successful room. And even though my living room is small, I treat it like a drawing room, with big scale and proportion being extremely important. And of course, I had fun with it!"

Design by Harry Heissmann

WHIMSY

Big rooms call for big ideas and patterns, as is beautifully demonstrated by Australian designer Diane Bergeron: "I wanted to recreate the feel of a glamorous New York loft full of color and classic contemporary design, so I contrasted the industrial bones of the warehouse space with Technicolor hues and vivid patterns: it makes the environment feel so exciting."

Design by Diane Bergeron

"I purposely chose vibrant orange walls for this bedroom to balance out the old-lady furniture," says
Mary McDonald. The shell-encrusted pelmets which, along with the
wavy curves of the headboard and valances, (not to mention the miniature ship painting cleverly hung on
the bed curtain) suggest dreams of exotic sea voyages.

Design by Mary McDonald

"My goal in creating my bedroom was to be happy in it," says photographer Oberto Gili, who used bold strokes of color and oversized scale to convey the pleasure and passion for the things he loves. Of particular note is the indulgence in hanging his beloved objects exactly where it best pleases him, which makes the space not only look beautiful, but feel deeply personal.

Design by Oberto Gili

Design by Philip Gorrivan

Seen one president, seen them all.

Set against black velvet walls, a bar area can have all the panache of a nightclub and you never have to leave home. Here, a punchy black-and-white photograph lends whimsy to an area distinctly created for having a drink and a swing.

Design by Philip Gorrivan

When it came time to wallpaper his kitchen, Jeffrey Alan Marks customized the pattern by having the fish swim all in one direction, their aquatic unity thereby giving the wall a cohesive yet still free-flowing feeling, which pairs perfectly with the creamy appeal of hand-waxed oak.

Design by Jeffrey Alan Marks

"Because this is a beach house, the pair of lobster lamps are a kitschy nod to the location," says designer Kevin Isbell. To fill the void underneath the table, Isbell took a large piece of driftwood that was in his client's outdoor shower and made it a focal point indoors: "I needed to fill the space with something compelling."

Design by Kevin Isbell

WHIMSY

Kathryn Ireland reminds us that bedrooms don't have to be soft and pastel-colored to feel dreamy. Here, the flower power of richly colored Suzani textiles and artwork creates indelible drama when paired with an imposing bed. "There is something about having posts that lends a sense of importance to a bedroom," says Ireland.

Design by Kathryn Ireland

A collection doesn't have to be expensive to bring visual significance to a wall.
"I've spent entirely too many hours of my life trolling eBay for oversized skeleton keys," says Jonathan
Adler. "They have such fab shapes and look very graphic on a wall."

Design by Jonathan Adler

WHIMSY

For the guest room in his lake cottage, Thom Filicia kept the décor simple yet lively by combining the
exotic textures of a batik bedspread and a contrasting curtain (without worrying
that it wouldn't go) against cream-colored walls. The vintage animal prints—elegantly clustered in threes—
are a unique and economical way to bring ornamentation to an important area.

Design by Thom Filicia

The Novogratz are never lazy with their spaces: they make the most out of every room by filling it with interesting, irregular finds from the floor straight up to the lighting fixture. Nothing feels too precious, yet everything is dear and, therefore, interesting.

Design by The Novogratz

WHIMSY

Within her small apartment, Elizabeth Pyne needed to somehow carve out space for a dining area, so she chose a glass-topped table with a perforated metal base to create a light casual feel. When combined with the branch-like forms of the Rene Prou chairs and the flower and butterfly wallpaper, the room has a cohesiveness that still transports its dwellers. "When I am working at the table," says Pyne, "I imagine I am sitting on a bench in the Luxembourg gardens in Paris."

Design by Elizabeth Pyne and Ann Pyne

WHIMSY

"I wanted to create a rustic yet modern, earthy vibe," says Julie Carlson, who arranged a trio of branch "antlers" mounted on handmade plaques in such a way as to accentuate and articulate the grand, slanted ceiling of her room without overwhelming it.

Design by Julie Carlson

A sense of life springs up from the energy provided by contrasts," says Maureen Footer. "Here, against the understated Dior Gray used for the walls, the spring yellow and parrot green truly pop." Footer anchors the elegant mix with a 1920s bust because: "over-scaled objects always look confident and anchor a room beautifully."

Design by Maureen Footer

"This living room was really just a shack by the sea," says Todd Alexander Romano, who designed and lived in it for some summers on Southampton. "It was a very small space and so I wanted it to be colorful and happy. I also wanted to use old-fashioned elements like the wicker porch chair, the painted tole sconces and the straw stools to give it a casual and easy air. Blurring the lines between indoor and outdoor was very important due to its tiny proportions!"

Design by Todd Alexander Romano

Tessa Pimontel and Hans Neleman were inspired not only by modern hotel design but also the principles of symmetry and harmony found in monasteries. An old hotel balcony grate above the charismatic four-poster bed gives the room extra personality.

Design by Tessa Pimontel

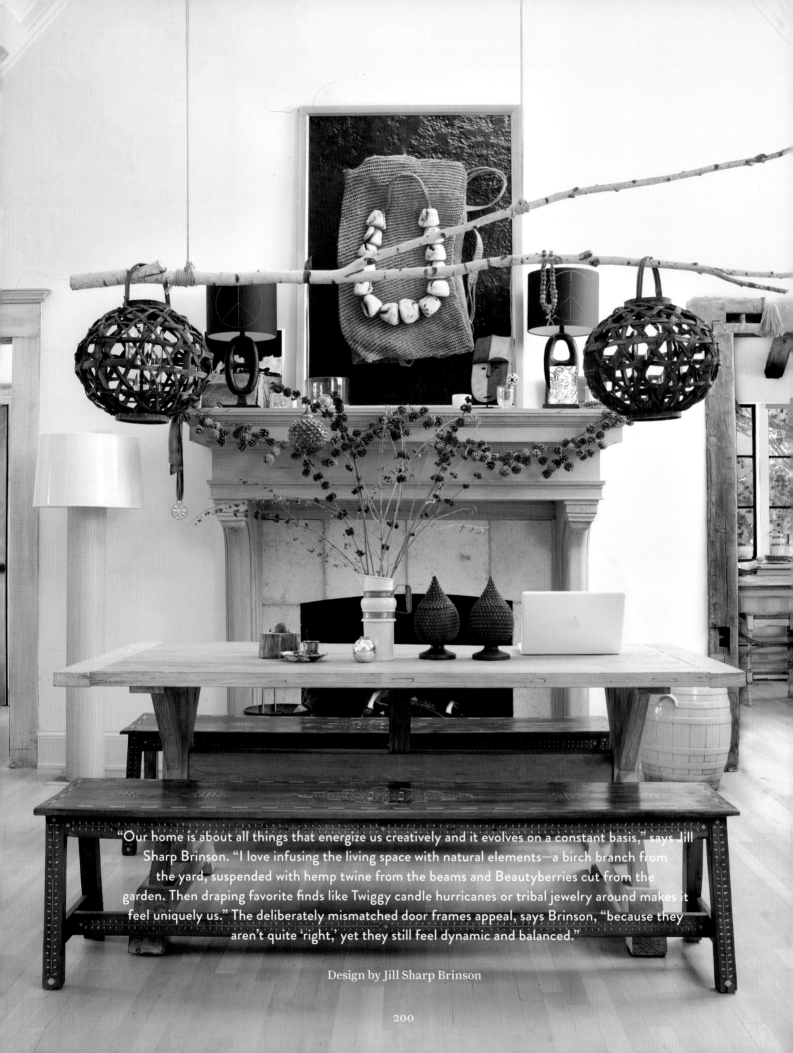

Design by Jill Sharp Brinson

"Our home is about all things that energize us creatively and it evolves on a constant basis," says Jill Sharp Brinson. "I love infusing the living space with natural elements—a birch branch from the yard, suspended with hemp twine from the beams and Beautyberries cut from the garden. Then draping favorite finds like Twiggy candle hurricanes or tribal jewelry around makes it feel uniquely us." The deliberately mismatched door frames appeal, says Brinson, "because they aren't quite 'right,' yet they still feel dynamic and balanced."

Design by Jill Sharp Brinson

Spacious amounts of white plaster wall allow the layered-in moments of this cozy sitting area to really pop. "I often choose a single powerful color, like the fuchsia of these peonies and then pick it up in a textile thrown over the arm of a chair," says owner Jill Sharp Brinson. Random textiles are often hung over the railing to further infuse whimsy, pattern and vibe into the room. "It's the equivalent of a adding an amazing accessory to your outfit," she says.

WHIMSY

Design by Jill Sharp Brinson

201

Introducing a picnic-style table and bench to one half of the family eating equation is genius, because it gives a country casual appeal to this city apartment's setting. The unexpectedly modern twist of the children's portraits and a spiffy white chandelier offer stylish color counterpoints.

Design by Amanda Nisbet

Don't let a thing like budget—or pictures, for that matter—stop you when it comes to transforming a space: try a décor that dares to be different. The bold combination of black and white on the bed spread gives instant oomph to a small space and is easily duplicated with a little paint and imagination onto the walls.

Accessorizing

You wouldn't leave home without the right shoes
or sunglasses, so don't allow your rooms to lack the
details that help articulate its personality

You wouldn't dream of leaving the house without the right shoes or jewelry. Your home should be equally distinguished, for the right accessories make the space feel wholly yours. It starts with a rug, which—like shoes—sets the room's mood as well as uniting its disparate elements. (Designers talk about the ceiling as a room's fifth wall; I'd like to argue that the floor is its sixth and should never be underestimated in its need to be properly adorned.) Curtains I think of in the same way I do a sweater: chosen not just for warmth and coverage, but for the ability to add an extra dimension of texture and color to the overall ensemble. For finishing touches, artwork, pillows and even end tables can amp up the glam factor much in the way jewelry does.

Manhattan designer Eric Cohler beautifully accessorizes a unique fireplace (p. 209) by making sure that every piece surrounding it—from the feminine portrait and nearby cluster of Starburst Mirrors to the whimsically shaped and upholstered sofa—manages to be both arresting and delicate.

In Annie Brahler's living room (pp. 214-215), texture, color and surprise create a layered look as chic as it is casual, that *je ne sais quoi* feeling you get when you long to mimic a French woman's outfit but can't quite figure out how. And Kristin Gallipoli (p. 220) adds oomph to white walls by adding a textural sculpture that seems to flirt with the equally vivacious animal-print pillows below.

Accessorizing is

For a room to come alive, the placement of accessories should be as playful as the accessories themselves.

To make a smaller space appear spacious and dimensional, spread out different kinds of accessories in areas around a room.

A single accessory—such as a dramatic mirror or curtains—can provide as much impact as multiples grouped together in innovative ways.

Gather your most beloved accessories into a landscape over, under and on a table: it will summon people and invite them to linger.

Color, texture and pattern, when combined with even just a few accessories, are every captivating room's secret weapon.

Accessories should echo—and deepen—the mood of a room the way the right jewelry can make an outfit.

To make his 250-square-feet studio space feel larger, Stephen Shubel went shopping for many different mirrors, mirrors and light-colored objects to visually open it up. "The trick to hanging on a very large wall is to have more items than you need," says Shubel, who laid out all of the items on the floor first to get the perfect placement. "I like having many different shapes, sizes, textures, and things that have a sculptural look to add interest. Avoid too many flat and boxy shapes or it will become very boring."

Design by Stephen Shubel

Eric Cohler makes a wall come alive by first draping it in violet and then layering in the intricate curves and patterns of the fireplace mantel and the collected objects on top. The penetrating gaze from the girl in the painting dares you to pay attention only to her while the playful placement of the mirrors lures your attention elsewhere.

Design by Eric Cohler

It's easy to forget the elegant power of quiet color until you see it executed with such panache. Here, designer Gerrie Bremmermann gives many of the room's accessories—from the blue glazed walls and the Ivory swirls of the painting to the gentle sparkle of the crystal sconces—ample opportunity to reinforce and celebrate the elegant gray palette.

Design by Gerrie Bremmermann

Inspired by her love of nature, Amanda Seitz used its many incarnations to transform her smallish space into a multi-tasking area that resonates with whimsy: the driftwood coffee table, the white ceramic deer head and the octopus triptych, each becomes a focal point, and the occupied eye forgets about boundaries.

Design by Amanda Seitz

This tiny bungalow's collected look rich with history is achieved in equal parts innovation and whimsy. A gallery wall of vintage botanicals shows sheets of music torn from books found in a Brussels flea market, while an old church kneeler has found a new calling as an end table. French armchairs in brown velvet gather around a salvaged wood coffee table, and threads of pink add shots of glamour to the masculine hues.

Design by Annie Brahler

ACCESSORIZING

Nicky Haslam creates the feeling of a luxurious 17th-century parlor room by mixing comfortable seating with a variety of lush textures and sheens against the faux bois and lacquer-painted paneling. All the elements here quietly work together to make the space feel both intimate and special.

Design by Nicky Haslam

ACCESSORIZING

By combining the strong, masculine legs of tables and chairs with light-spirited artwork,
Robert Stilin and Waldo Fernandez create a living room that feels both grounded and ethereal.

Design by Robert Stilin and Waldo Fernandez

ACCESSORIZING

A white room can be serene and still feel glamorous when gold and beige are added to the equation with accessories that carry equal parts style and humor. "I had to bring life to a room with three plain walls and one wall with an enormous expanse of windows," says Kristin Gallipoli. "So I had the windows covered with one large panel of Belgian linen to block out the rising sun. The walls were painted almost white to give the room a modern feel. Then I kept the bedding simple. Custom-made animal print pillows were an inexpensive way to add life and pattern."

Design by Kristin Gallipoli

No matter your budget, you can create a memorable vignette against almost any wall in your home by taking inspiration from what designer Bunny Williams did here: place a table as a foundation below a mirror with personality. Add a pair of lamps and chairs on either side for balance and then have fun weaving in decorative pieces that you love or make you smile.

Design by Bunny Williams

ACCESSORIZING

"I use a lot of white and then layer in my artwork to my canvas," says Victoria Smith, who refers to her décor style as "mid-century meets bohemian modern. "Very few things in my home are brand new. I think vintage-inspired design is an extension of my personality: it's the kind of décor I feel most comfortable living with and feeds my creativity. I love collecting unique vintage pieces from lots of different genres and eras and mixing them all up to create an eclectic space that reflects my personal style."

Design by Victoria Smith

ACCESSORIZING

Wanting to create a warm modernist retreat for a family, designer Amy Lau played
up the luxuriously large windows by giving them a sense of sense of movement, thanks to
curtains dressed in an undulating, geometric, embroidered pattern.

Design by Amy Lau

When treasured pieces are edited and displayed with restraint, not only does the gathered collection deliver a powerful, stylish impact, but there's also room for the eye to take its time and delight in each. Designer Carol-Ann Speros enthuses: "Never overlook the common."

Design by Carol-Ann Speros

This bedroom offers a fearless compilation of like-minded color, texture and pattern that all work together to create a room full of depth and comfort. Inspired by the natty suits of fashion designer Thom Browne, designer Jay Jeffers created the custom tartan platform bed. The tailored headboard stylishly anchors the ethereal wall arches, which were painted right over the moldings and baseboards to make the room feel even more expansive.

Design by Jay Jeffers

Alex Papachristidis creates luxurious dimension and texture on a simple wall by placing gold-accented wall pieces against richly patterned wallpaper with the aplomb of donning fine jewels.

Design by Alex Papachristidis

ACCESSORIZING

Wanting to play bold color and pattern off the soft gray walls, Summer Thornton decided to frame a wallpaper pattern she loved, rather than go the traditional artwork route. "It's a fun and fresh way to bring wallpaper into the space without going wall-to-wall and floor-to-ceiling," says Thornton, who added another unexpected element by using a file cabinet as a side table for its function and modernity.

Design by Summer Thornton

When Martyn Lawrence-Bullard's client wanted their ranch in Santa Fe to feel more sophisticated than typically Southwestern, Lawrence-Bullard distressed the walls with natural pigments to create the illusion of age and then framed the vast windows with billowing raw silk. "This toned them down," explains Lawrence-Bullard. The ceiling beams are reclaimed railway ties left in their original patina for added atmosphere. "Overall the palette is warm and inviting, with its distressed red leather and burnt umber upholstery, and the artworks give the place a feeling of modernity."

Design by Martyn Lawrence-Bullard

Rule-breaking

The rules we cling to are all too often the very elements that keep a room from looking fabulous

Breaking the rules of good design isn't about deciding to forgo furniture or comfort. All of the rooms that follow are real, lived-places, with style cleverly arranged into their DNA. But these spaces don't simply settle for looking good. Gestures that at first seem to defy Design 101 with unusual uses of color, scale, balance or placement, break through that design ceiling we all instinctively—and often mistakenly—place too low over our heads. 'We shouldn't go there,' we remind ourselves over and over like a bad mantra. But thankfully, the designers and owners who follow did go there.

The designers here fly without fear or a safety net and the results may challenge those ideas you thought would have ended up a design disaster: Shouldn't curtains framing enormous windows be as unobtrusively patterned as possible so as not to overwhelm the room? Not to famed New York designer Muriel Brandolini (p. 242). For her client's apartment she designed an oversized pattern of squares in warm browns and currant so unique, that instead of suffocating the space, it envelops its visitors like a chic cocoon. Tori Mellott's striped living room (p. 248), punctuated with her beloved artwork hung more via whimsy than symmetry, vibrates with life instead of chaos when confidence is the measuring tape.

None of these rooms break actual rules, but rather misconceptions born from our fear of getting something wrong. So let these examples prove that there really is no wrong. Perhaps some of them will at first make you feel slightly uncomfortable. But don't turn the page too soon: rather, allow the room's unique spirit to settle over you, allowing your eye to acclimate to its unexpectedness.

By showing us that the sky is the limit, these rooms offer a whole new palette of possibility. Not only will you likely pluck an idea or two for your own space, but by watching the masters walk the tight rope between disaster and sensation, you might also realize that there isn't as far to fall as you first imagined.

Rule-breaking is

Who says that your artwork must be of the same era as the antique it is hung over!

Sometimes a room comes to life not as a result of what you put in, but when you take away what's expected.

Rooms don't have to do just one thing, so why can't a dining room also be a library or a kitchen also be a showcase for collections?

A surfboard in a kitchen? Vertical stripes in a living room? Placing things where you least expect them brings elegant excitement to a space.

Use color to break the so-called rules: a turquoise backsplash in a kitchen or a dining room wrapped in dark navy prove that being a little naughty is nice.

The mood of a room doesn't always have to mirror its surroundings: why not create a city vibe in the country or a country vibe in the city?

"People keep asking us when the rug is arriving," says Nancy Pyne of the living room she and legendary designer Albert Hadley worked to create in her new home. "And they can't believe it when I tell them never." "We wanted the house to feel very light," says Hadley. "And with the floors painted an expansive white it simply didn't need it."

Design by Albert Hadley

RULE-BREAKING

In Annie Brahler's own snug kitchen, a peacock finds the ideal perch on a Tiffany-Blue Frigidaire while a former buffet with its cabinet doors changed out for drawers is transformed into an island. Never underestimate the effect of a glamorous lighting fixture in the kitchen; this one feels both intentional and spontaneous.

Design by Annie Brahler

Designer Alex Papachristidis understands it's in the playful tension of juxtaposing the old with the new that great decorating can be found. Too much of one thing (no matter how beautiful) and the eye tires. Here, a precious antique gets renewed vigor when placed beneath the surprise pop of modern artwork.

Design by Alex Papachristidis

RULE BREAKING

Wall treatments can add an invaluable dimension to wall décor. Here, a painterly backdrop of gray and white sets off a pair of powerful images smartly framed in corresponding white.

Design by The Novogratz

Why can't a dining room be more like a library and vice versa? This duality can be an ideal solution not only for avid readers but also those who wish to bring more intimacy to their formal eating areas, which so often feel more cold than chic. An over-the-top lighting fixture connects both worlds beautifully by looking studious and glamorous.

Design by Peter Dunham

Designer Julie Hillman understands that sometimes a piece of art transcends its usual function by not just bringing beauty to a room but by becoming a visual pull that dares you to look away. She smartly lets the rest of the space defer to that power by keeping it clean and spare.

Design by Julie Hillman

RULE-BREAKING

Muriel Brandolini understands that big rooms require big gestures to emphasize their greatness. But instead of crowding the space, she keeps the drama contained at the windows and then extends the bold pattern from the ground up to make one soaring statement.

Design by Muriel Brandolini

"I wanted a table—not an island—for this kitchen, which was a little controversial given that islands in kitchens are so ubiquitous," says designer Thomas Smythe. He also gave a nod to the coziness of old-fashioned country brick kitchen floors by using a classic herringbone pattern but dressed it up for its city location with black slate. An over-scaled lantern adds soul and just the right note of unexpected formality.

Design by Thomas Smythe

After a cement truck slipped down the hillside and landed in this Malibu kitchen, the entire space had to be rebuilt. The task was to recreate a space that celebrated the family's love for art, animals and surfing. The kitchen table is like a picnic bench and reflects their casual lifestyle.

Design by Maxine Greenspan

A dining area at the other end of an open-plan living room is given its own personality in order to feel distinct. A bookshelf contains a beloved collection of pottery that is displayed as prominently as artwork. "I think living only with pieces you love is important," says their owner Raina Kattelson, who complemented the arrangement with a lively lighting fixture. "I wanted something that would be dramatic but at the same time light and airy so as not to darken the space."

Design by Raina Kattelson

Ruthie Sommers gave a breakfast room for young children the happy spirit of an ice cream parlor (complete with brown-and-white stripes on the wall) and the chic punch of Hollywood Regency style. "To get just the right colors for the chairs we chose clothing linen and then laminated it," says Sommers. "It was inexpensive and added the fun pop. And the children got to pick which chair color they want to sit on."

Design by Ruthie Sommers

"Rather than hang one enormous artwork, I like to anchor a collage over the sofa with a large convex mirror, which also maximizes light," says Tori Mellott of the big-effect strokes able to draw inside a nearly 450-square-foot space. "The pieces help set the dramatic stage as well as emphasize the high ceiling."

Design by Tori Mellott

RULE-BREAKING

Dark walls combined with the bright white of the ceiling and fireplace bring an
unexpected formality to a dining room that—thanks to mismatched mid-century finds—also manages to
feel casually festive. One look at the glamorous flokati rug combined with the honey
wood floors will make you reconsider the Oriental standby. "I'm not afraid to jump in and try things,"
says owner and self-professed flea market queen Victoria Smith. "I want my rooms to have a sense of
humor but also to feel mature."

Design by Victoria Smith

For their own Connecticut living room, designers Linda Zelenko and Stephen Piscuskas wanted casual country living that didn't sacrifice city sleekness. "We envisioned and crafted every element of the environment," says Zelenko. "From the leather walls to the custom furniture, every texture and tone had to have an elegant sophistication, as well as feel like an extension of the countryside. Most of all, we wanted the space to make people feel relaxed."

Design by Linda Zelenko and Stephen Piscuskas

One look at this Diamond Baratta designed kitchen for a house on the Gulf of Mexico and you'll wonder
why you played it so safe with yours. The turquoise back splash and
the lime green and blue glass pendants infuse a unique vitality within while accentuating
the hues of the ocean and lush lawns outside. "Sometimes the best answer to coloring
a decorating project is bringing the outside environment in," says Anthony Baratta.

Design by Diamond Baratta

By mixing rich tones of wood, designer Vicente Wolf is able to give his clients a kitchen
that feels both spacious and inviting. The substitution of a dining room table instead
of an island is an unexpected touch, which warms up the modern, utilitarian feel of the shelves and
counters and beckons diners to gather and enjoy a well-prepared meal.

Design by Vicente Wolf

A 1930s cottage is transformed into a grand space via an oversized dining table and chandelier found in Mexico. The brick chimney is casually covered with paintings from the owners' Dutch and Belgian families: an elegant way to personalize a space without getting too serious.

Design by Tessa Pimontel

"I'm a fan of using utilitarian furniture pieces in lieu of manufactured cabinetry in a kitchen," says designer Darryl Carter, who used an 18th-century Italian table with a worn top as an island in his own weekend retreat. Carter's use of a primitive door and lots of white makes the house feel both modern and warmly rustic. "There is," he rightly declares, "no substitute for actual wear."

Design by Darryl Carter

For a dining room transformed into a spacious library and television viewing space for a family, red was chosen not only because it feels cozy but because of the stylish punch it gives. The custom checkered rug expertly brings the color into the rest of the room without showing off. People are so often afraid to use strong colors and this room is a great example of why you shouldn't be.

Design by Diamond Baratta

With its distressed leather chairs, lacquered Parsons Table and shell chandelier, this Connecticut dining room has all the glamour of a city penthouse yet—thanks to its oak panels, wood floors and expansive country views—still remains true to its environment.

Design by Linda Zelenko and Stephen Piscuskas

Designer Credits

Jonathan Adler
Balance, pp. 156–157; Whimsy, p. 189
www.jonathanadler.com

Thomas Beeton
Color, p. 53
Thomas M. Beeton + Associates
www.beetonassociates.com

Diane Bergeron
Color, p. 46; Whimsy, p. 181
Diane Bergeron Interiors
www.dianebergeron.com

Nate Berkus
Mix, p. 99
Nate Berkus Associates
www.nateberkusdesign.com

Carol Bokuniewicz
Color, pp. 38–39; Mix, p. 66
www.carolbdesign.com

Annie Brahler
Accessorizing, pp. 214–215;
Rule-breaking, p. 236
Euro Trash
www.euro-trash.us

Alessandra Branca
Color, pp. 50–51
www.branca.com

Muriel Brandolini
Rule-breaking, p. 242
www.murielbrandolini.com

Gerrie Bremermann
Accessorizing, pp. 210–211
Bremermann Designs
www.bremermanndesigns.com

Jill Sharp Brinson
Whimsy, pp. 200–201
www.jillsharpstyle.com

Kristen Buckingham
Arrangement, pp. 122–123
Kristen Buckingham Interior Design
www.kristenbuckingham.com

Betsy Burnham
Color, pp. 40–41; Balance, pp.
148–149
Burnham Design
www.burnhamdesign.com

Julie Carlson
Whimsy, p. 194
www.remodelista.com

**Carrier and Company
Interiors, Ltd.**
Color, pp. 36–37
www.carrierandcompany.com

Darryl Carter
Mix, p. 83; Arrangement, p. 128;
Rule-breaking, p. 258
www.darrylcarter.com

Eric Cohler
Accessorizing, p. 209
Eric Cohler Design
www.ericcohler.com

**Paul Costello and
Sara Ruffin Costello**
Mix, pp. 60–61
www.paulcostello.net

Robert Couturier
Balance, pp. 144–145
Robert Couturier & Associates
www.robertcouturier.com

Curated
Balance, p. 155
www.curated.com

Elizabeth Daugherty
Arrangement, p. 118

Milly de Cabrol
Mix, pp. 84–85
Milly de Cabrol, Ltd.
www.millydecabrol.com

Jan Showers
Balance, p. 147, 162
www.janshowers.com

Stephen Shubel
Cover; Mix, pp. 58–59;
Accessories, p. 208
Stephen Shubel Design, Inc.
www.stephenshubeldesign.com

Victoria Smith
Accessories, pp. 222–223;
Rule-breaking, p. 249
www.sfgirlbybay.com

Windsor Smith
Balance, pp. 142–143
Windsor Smith Home
www.windsorsmithhome.com

Matthew Patrick Smyth
Mix, pp. 96–97;
Arrangement, pp. 106–107
Matthew Patrick Smyth
Interior Design
www.matthewsmyth.com

Thomas Smythe
Rule-breaking, p. 243
Sarah Richardson Design
www.sarahrichardsondesign.com

Ruthie Sommers
Rule-breaking, p. 247
Ruthie Chapman Sommers
Interior Design
www.ruthiesommers.com

Carol-Ann Speros
Balance, pp. 166–167;
Accessorizing, p. 225
casperos@mac.com

Robert Stilin
Mix, p. 98;
Accessorizing, pp. 218–219
Robert Stilin, LLC
www.robertstilin.com

Jane Stubbs
Arrangement, p. 134
www.janestubbs.com

Rose Tarlow
Color, pp. 28–29
Rose Tarlow Melrose House
www.rosetarlow.com

Summer Thornton
Accessorizing, p. 228
Summer Thornton Design
www.summerthorntondesign.com

Melissa Warner
Color, p. 30–31
Massucco Warner Miller
www.massuccowarner
millerinteriordesign.com

Kelly Wearstler
Whimsy, pp. 176–177
www.kellywearstler.com

Amie Weitzman
Arrangement, pp. 108–109, 130–131
Amie Weitzman Interior Design
www.amieweitzman.com

Kendall Wilkinson
Whimsy, pp. 178–179
Kendall Wilkinson Design
www.kendallwilkinsondesign.com

Bunny Williams
Color, pp. 18–19; Accessories, p. 221
www.bunnywilliams.com

Caitlin Wilson
Arrangment, p. 112
Caitlin Wilson Design
www.caitlinwilsoninteriordesign.com

Vicente Wolf
Rule-Breaking, pp. 254–255
Vicente Wolf Associates, Inc.
www.vicentewolf.com

**Linda Zelenko and
Stephen Piscuskas**
Rule-Breaking, pp. 250-251; 260-261
York Street Studio
www.yorkstreet.com

Fabric Credits

Title page, p. 2
Raja Embroidery
by Martyn Lawrence-Bullard for Schumacher

Contents page, p. 4
Adras Ikat
by Martyn Lawrence-Bullard for Schumacher

Color, p.14
Foreground: Dragone
by Dedar
Background: Kochi Kashmir
by John Robshaw Textiles

Mix, p. 54
Foreground: Nankin
by Manuel Canovas
Background: Kashmir Paisley
from Peter Dunham Textiles

Arrangement, p. 102
Foreground: Baldwin Bamboo
by Scalamandre
Background: Shanghai
by Scalamandre

Balance, p. 138
Foreground: The Lotus Papers
by Farrow & Ball
Background: Broad Stripe
by Farrow & Ball

Whimsy, p. 170
Foreground: paradiso in panama
by fromental
Background: Black Mu Ikat
by Madeline Weinrib

Accessorizing, p. 204
Foreground: Belfort
by Manuel Canovas available through Cowtan & Tout
Background: Scarlett
by Manuel Canovas available through Cowtan & Tout

Rule-Breaking, p. 230
Foreground: Peony
by Katie Ridder Inc.
Background: Tortuga
by Manuel Canovas available through Cowtan & Tout

Photography Credits

Acknowledgments

Profuse and indebted thanks to all the extraordinary designers featured in this book. Not just for so generously giving me your glorious images without hesitation, but for your inspiring and insightful ideas. Every day I learn more from you. Thank you for making the world a more beautiful—and functional—place.

Rizzoli continues to welcome me under their gracious and glittering roof and I am the luckier.

Ellen Nidy, you are an editor who feels as much a friend as a mentor—not to mention copilot!

A special shout out to photographer Patrick Cline for lending me some of my most favorite rooms from *Lonny Magazine*. And also to photographers John Gruen, Pieter Estersohn and Tim Street-Porter for their artful eyes and keener patience.

And to my amazing husband and boys: Wherever we are is always home.

First published in the United States of America in 2012 by

Rizzoli International Publications, Inc.

300 Park Avenue South, New York, NY 10010

www.rizzoliusa.com

Book design: Allison Williams / Design MW www.designmw.com

Design Coordinator: Kayleigh Jankowski

2012 2013 2014 2015 2016 / 10 9 8 7 6 5 4

ISBN-13: 978-0-8478-3844-8

Library of Congress Control Number: 2011941707

Printed and bound in China

Distributed to the U.S. trade by Random House